Kings Park Festival

Festival

WA Botanic Garden

Kings Park

Wildflower Festival

It is spring.

We like to go for a walk in spring.

5

Look at the flowers.

We can see

the blue flowers.

8

We can see

the yellow flowers.

We can see

the red flowers.

13

We can see

the pink flowers.

We can see

all the flowers in spring.